THE HERALD BOOK OF THE CLYDE

THE HERALD BOOK OF
THE CLYDE

ROBERT JEFFREY & IAN WATSON

First published 1998
by B&W Publishing Ltd, Edinburgh
ISBN 1 873631 88 X
Copyright © Scottish Media Newspapers
Introduction copyright © Robert Jeffrey & Ian Watson

British Library Cataloguing Publication Data:
A catalogue record for this book is available
from the British Library.

Copies of many of the photographs in this book
are available for personal or commercial use.
Contact: Photo Sales Department,
Scottish Media Newspapers,
195 Albion Street, Glasgow, G1 1QP,
quoting the picture reference number.

Printed in Glasgow by Caledonian International Book Manufacturing

INTRODUCTION

To a youngster from Croftfoot on Glasgow's southside the Clyde was a magical barrier to be crossed on the way to town. A barrier that presented hours of delight watching the Broomielaw dredgers at work or the cargo boats loading and unloading at Clyde Street, right in the heart of the city. Or better still a trip on the Govan Ferry.

Further down the river for a boy from Knightswood, on the northside, the Clyde was just as dominant, but different. Here you were within earshot of the sounds of the yards whose cranes dotted the horizon. Even on the way to school you could see the great ships take shape.

A love of the Clyde came with the territory.

Travel up-river from the city and stand on the gentle hills around Elvanfoot looking up the Daer Valley. You are looking at the Clyde's birthplace. But not the exact birthplace.

There is no one definite source. The water that runs off those impressive, undulating Lanarkshire hills joins the Daer, the Potrail and the Clydes Burn before flowing down to the Firth of Clyde and Ailsa Craig.

The Clyde is not a mighty river. It is no Amazon or Mississippi, yet it enjoys worldwide fame and affection unmatched by any other Scottish river. In this book we have tried to capture the character of the river and of the people along its banks, their industries, their recreations, their wealth, their poverty, their successes and setbacks.

From its uncertain source in the southern uplands to one of the most scenic Firths in the world, the river has inspired poets and painters.

In the upper reaches, in the days before the Falls of Clyde were harnessed to generate hydro-electric power, Bonnington Linn and Corra Linn inspired William Turner and William Wordsworth and provided the setting for Sir Walter Scott's *Old Mortality*. Further downstream near Hamilton, in more recent times the river was diverted to help create Strathclyde Loch, a popular venue for sailing and rowing events.

The saying "the Clyde made Glasgow and Glasgow made the Clyde" might be hackneyed, but it captures the essence of the middle reaches. In the eighteenth century, extensive engineering works were necessary to deepen the channel to allow Glasgow to flourish as a sea port. The shipbuilders of Scotstoun, Govan, Linthouse, Clydebank, Port Glasgow and Greenock made "Clydebuilt" a byword for quality.

The outsider might find it difficult to comprehend how liners of such elegance and beauty could emerge from the apparent chaos of the shipyard, its scaffolding crawling with tradesmen practising a plethora of skills, many now forgotten. The names of the yards—Stephen, Connell, Fairfield, Barclay Curle, Yarrow, John Brown, Denny, Scott and Lithgow—are etched in history.

Today the Glasgow waterfront—despite the temporary fillip of the 1988 Garden Festival, the recent arrival of the Armadillo and the conversion of the Renfrew Ferry to a popular concert venue—unfortunately struggles to become a focus for urban life. Sculptor George Wyllie's imaginative creations—the paper boat and the straw locomotive on the Finnieston crane—serve as periodic reminders that the river can and should be a centrepiece.

The Finnieston crane itself still stands proud and symbolic, whilst similar giant structures, like those of General Terminus Quay, have been swept away by changing times.

Changing times that have seen the Conference Centre rise on derelict dockland, and the Kingston and Erskine bridges spell the end for famous ferry crossings.

Beyond the Tail of the Bank, the estuary is joined by numerous sea lochs which cut into the mountains of Argyll and the Cowal peninsula, a spectacular and challenging lure for sailing enthusiasts.

But even here there have been good times and bad times.

The US Polaris submarine base at the Holy Loch was the focus for CND protests during the years of the Cold War and helped bolster the economy of Dunoon which had been largely deserted by holiday-makers seeking the sun of the Spanish Costas. Eventually the US Navy sailed home and the area now works at rebuilding its tourism.

Many of these evocative photographs from the magnificent archives of *The Herald* and *Evening Times* recall the halcyon days for resorts like Rothesay, Largs, Ayr and Prestwick, when the estuary was a playground for the people of the Clydeside conurbation, and a fleet of passenger steamers ploughed up and down the river and to and fro across the firth. A fleet now reduced to a sole survivor, the *Waverley*.

Everyone who has lived on the banks of the Clyde, or stood on the shores of the firth, has a different memory of the river. We hope a journey through these pages will rekindle yours, or open new windows to one of the world's great rivers.

RJ & IW

ACKNOWLEDGEMENTS

This book is a tribute to the skill and dedication of
The Herald and *Evening Times* staff photographers
down the years, whose work has produced
one of the world's greatest picture archives.

The assistance of the following people in the
preparation of this book is gratefully acknowledged:
Lois Munro, Donny O'Rourke and the staff of
The Herald and Evening Times Picture Library—
Malcolm Beaton, Jim McNeish, Tony Murray,
Ben Adams and Catherine Turner.

FROM SOURCE TO CITY

1. Sunlight sparkles on the fledgling Clyde as a Clydesdale horse, that sturdy symbol of the West of Scotland, grazes on a riverside meadow near Elvanfoot. Up-river, in the background, are the Lowther Hills, from which flow the waters that become the Clyde. It is difficult to pinpoint its exact source, but this view shows the river near the beginning of its long run to the sea.

2 & 3. Even a few miles from the headwaters, industry makes its mark. The majestic Falls of Clyde have been a famous source of inspiration for artists down the years. Despite their beauty—captured in watercolour by Turner and in verse by Wordsworth—a Government report in 1928 stated that the nation could no longer afford to waste the national resources of mineral wealth or water power and there was political pressure to create hydro-electric schemes. The power station at Corra Linn is seen during its construction in the late 1930s and on completion.

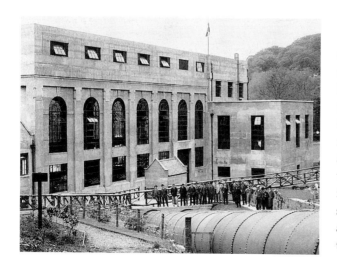

4 *(opposite)*. Winter bites hard in the rural stretches of the upper Clyde. In 1991, frost and plummeting temperatures only just failed to tame the Clyde at Corra Linn, the river's progress reduced to little more than a trickle amidst the snow and icicles. The waterfall is at its most dramatic for only five days in the year, when the power station is closed for engineering works, allowing the full force to cascade over the 80-foot drop.

5, 6 & 7 (*opposite*). New life has now been breathed into New Lanark, which had become an almost forgotten ghost-town. Now a popular tourist attraction, this visionary industrial village, created by Robert Owen, attracts more than 100,000 visitors a year. For around 200 years, visitors from Europe and Russia flocked to New Lanark to view the mills and the innovative production techniques but, by the time the Gourock Ropeworks Company closed the last of the mills in 1968, the outlook was bleak. However, a gradual process of restoration began, the village came alive again and many homes were beautifully restored. The old mills became popular attractions, with fairs and car rallies adding to the fun. The development has continued in recent years and, in May 1998, the New Lanark Mill Hotel opened in what is now recognised as a heritage site of worldwide importance.

ERECTED BY THE CO-OPERATORS OF
LANARKSHIRE IN COMMEMORATION
OF ROBERT OWEN, WHO IN THESE
PREMISES CARRIED OUT HIS TRADING
EXPERIMENT IN SOCIAL REFORM
1800 - 1824

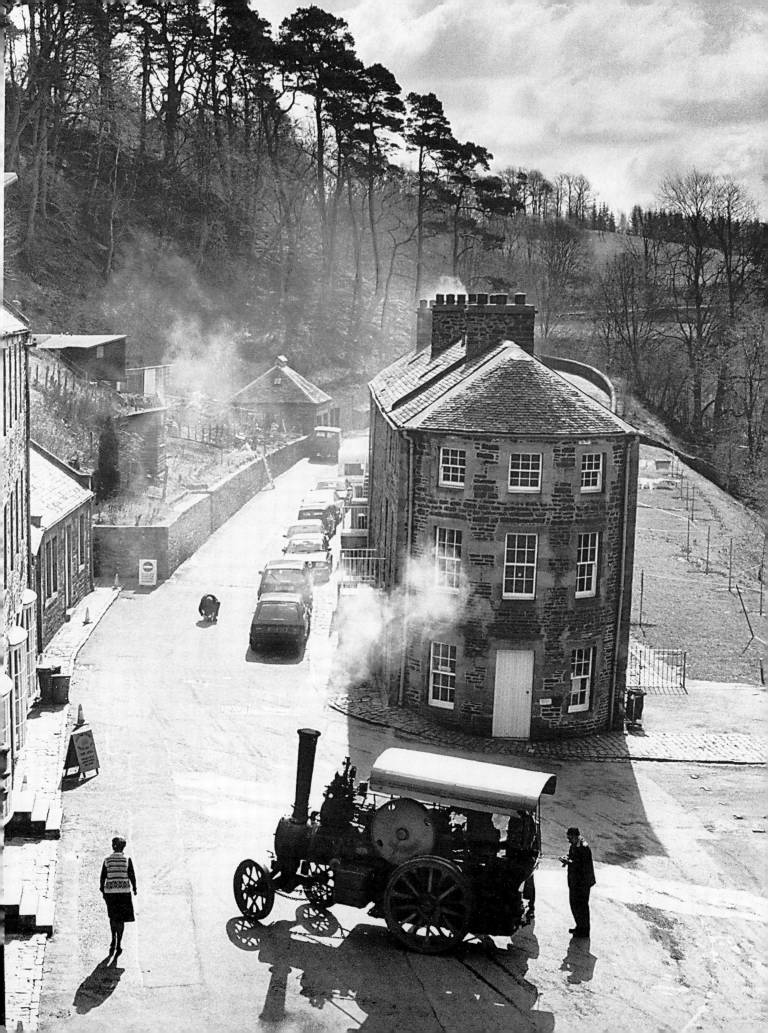

8 & 9. Lanark, an elegant old burgh and important market town, sits high above the River Clyde. These two photographs of Lanimer Day, taken 48 years apart (1934 and 1982), prove that the enjoyment of this traditional ritual endures. They were taken from similar viewpoints, looking up High Street: the bunting seemingly unchanged, the fashions wildly different. This annual fair, which takes place in June, is based on the Riding of the Marches—inspection of the burgh boundary marker stones. The festivities are something that no self-respecting inhabitant of Lanark would wish to miss and are as memorable to the bowler-hatted riders as they are to the children and to the Lanimer Queen.

10 & 11. Lanark Racecourse, which dates back to the seventeenth century, was also home to Ewing's School of Flying, founded in 1911. The previous year had seen Scotland's first flying meeting at which one of the performers, James Radley, demonstrated his Bleriot-type aircraft. There has been no horse racing at Lanark since 1977.

12. Claimed to be the world's oldest horse-racing trophy, the Silver Bell—made in Edinburgh in the early seventeenth century—is seen here (background left) as part of an exhibition in 1955.

14. Coal-mining was an important industry in the Clyde valley. These Lanarkshire miners are quoted in the original caption as being "pleased with the result of government negotiations" in the aftermath of the First World War.

15. Life in the mining villages was rough and ready in the old days. A house-wife empties out the slops—a daily chore. No chrome baths or waste disposal units in those days!

13 (*opposite*). Whuppity Scoorie is a fun-filled Lanark tradition which takes place at 6pm on 1 March each year. This custom requires the local children to run round the St Nicholas Church three times, while whirling a ball of tightly packed paper at the end of a piece of string! The church bells ring to warn demons away.

16. Experienced eyes weigh up the worth of black-faced rams in the sixties. The Lanark Auction Market has for generations been a huge attraction for the farming community in the area, the excitement of market day spilling over into pubs galore as farmers enjoyed a day away from their chores.

17. Mining was not Lanarkshire's only industry. In the 1950s, in a 200-year-old tannery, said to be Scotland's oldest, Lanarkshire men haul hides out of a lime bath in the leather-making process. Back-breaking work.

18. In and around Kirkfieldbank the fertile valley was exploited by fruit farms and orchards in the nineteenth century, generating considerable wealth, particularly from tomato growing. Eventually, cheap imports hit the famous Scotch tomatoes. The area is still popular for day trips, especially in May and June when the countryside is a blaze of pink blossoms. The valley has many nurseries, most with coffee shops to provide day-trippers with scones—and the opportunity to buy plants! Garrion Bridge is a famous landmark on this stretch of the river.

19. In the upper reaches the Crossford Raft Race was a source of fun for competitors and spectators alike. The essence of the race is captured in this shot of the "Silver Dream Machine" in September 1991. That year, the race was postponed because the river had risen dangerously. The "Machine" did, however, make a run from Hazelbank to Overton Farm.

20. Not exactly a riverbank sight, but this iron horse is symbolic of the mighty Clydesdale, a mixture of local packhorse mares and stallions, which emerged as a distinctive breed in the Clyde valley. The sculpture, erected in 1997, stands in Easterhouse Business Park. Sculptor Andrew Scott has dramatically caught the essence of this friendly breed.

21. Strathclyde Park is not only popular for water sports. The famous "T in the Park" pop festival took place here from 1994 to 1996, drawing huge crowds of pop fans of all ages from all parts of the country.

22. Chatelherault was designed in 1732 by William Adam as the hunting lodge of the fifth Duke of Hamilton. A multi-million pound restoration project started in the late seventies, and it is now popular for walks in the nearby woods and for children to play in the adventure park. It is also a much favoured venue for wedding receptions and, when floodlit, is a spectacular sight against the skyline. A much vaunted tale is that the fifth Duke used to tell visiting aristocrats that the magnificent structure was merely his "dog kennels".

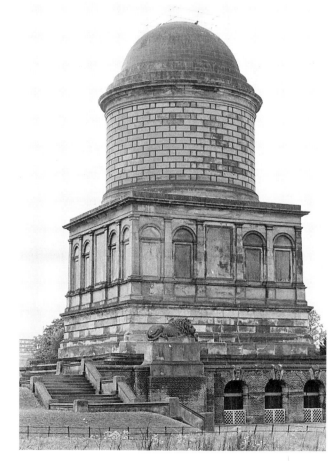

23. The Hamilton Mausoleum, built by the tenth Duke of Hamilton as a chapel and burial crypt, is prominent in the view from Chatelherault down to the river, although Hamilton Palace, the ancestral home of the Dukes, itself no longer exists. Unfortunately, the remarkable echo inside the Mausoleum made it unsuitable as a place of worship.

25. Ravenscraig in full production in the early eighties, the giant works dominating the landscape and showing how the very name of the plant became a by-word for industrial Scotland. It was opened by Colville Iron and Steel Company in 1957 and nationalised as part of British Steel in 1967. After many years of campaigning to save the plant, it was finally closed in 1992 with the loss of around 4000 jobs. At the time, it was estimated that a further 2000 jobs from the local economy would also be lost.

24 (*previous page*). This atmospheric picture taken virtually in the shadow of the giant Ravenscraig towers reflects the despair of steel workers at the plant who suffered years of anxiety and insecurity in the run-up to the closure. Despite the closure being widely predicted for years, there was still an enormous struggle to keep the plant open.

26. This scene from 1928 shows legendary missionary David Livingstone's birthplace at Blantyre before the tenement was restored to become a visitors' centre. Blantyre has long been a popular spot for Sunday School trips for the children of the Clyde valley. Livingstone worked in the local textile mills and went on to study Medicine at Glasgow University before embarking on missionary work in Africa.

27. A tableau from the visitors' centre, illustrating Livingstone's work.

28 & 29. Down-river from Blantyre is the town of Uddingston, home of the famous Tunnock's Caramel Wafer. This family-owned bakery is an institution in Glasgow and the West of Scotland. The name was prominent not only on gable ends as in the picture above but also on the famous fleet of red vans.

30. A little further down-river, on the eastern edge of Glasgow, this was the grim, industrial reality of the Clydebridge Steel Works in the 1930s. The iron and steel industry in this part of Glasgow was fuelled in the eighteenth century by local mines, and the East End districts of Tollcross and Auchenshuggle were at the centre of the industrial revolution: tobacco baron James Dunlop opened a pit near here in 1777, an investment which helped him ride out a recession in the tobacco business. In 1810 he further diversified by taking over the Clyde Iron Works.

31 & 32. The Royal Burgh of Rutherglen received its Royal Charter in the twelfth century. Despite the shallowness of the river at this point, Rutherglen was a busy port in the nineteenth century, sending coal down the river. It also boasted a thriving shipbuilding business, especially pleasure steamers and cluthas—passenger ferries—popular in the days before electric trams. Note the characteristic street scene complete with sun awnings and another creative use of the gable end, this time to advertise whisky. The Town Hall with its distinctive clock tower continues to dominate Main Street in this proud burgh.

THE CITY

33. More water sports—this time on the edge of Glasgow Green. This 1958 shot of Glasgow schools' rowing crews also shows the old buildings on the south side of the river, soon to be demolished as part of the Gorbals redevelopment.

34. Glasgow Green is famous for its knock-about football games, but this time the lads are playing cricket—dangerously close to the giant glass panels of the Winter Gardens!

35 & 36. Glasgow Green is also famous for its annual fair in July, seen here in full swing in 1971 (left). The Green has been used for various other fairs and attractions, everything from Michael Jackson concerts to soap box derbies, May Day rallies to marathons and, in 1998, big screen World Cup TV: in the *Evening Times* Tartan Tent these fans are joyous in defeat—again!

37. The river has its tragic side and, over the years, has claimed many lives. The task of recovering the bodies fell mainly to the legendary Ben Parsonage of the Glasgow Humane Society who, in his time, had the grim task of recovering more than 2000 bodies from the river. However, he also saved more than 300 from drowning. Ben worked on the river for more than 50 years before he died at the age of 76.

38. Ben's son, George, continues the family tradition, although with much improved equipment. He is in the *Sarah Parsonage* rescue boat out on the water with Lord Provost Robert Gray in 1986. Provost Gray is seated in one of Ben Parsonage's old dinghies. In the background is part of the Gorbals redevelopment.

39. Legendary Glasgow historian Jack House's favourite bridge over the Clyde was the St Andrew's, built in 1854 to allow workers to reach the many new industrial sites starting up on the south side of the city. This 1949 view shows the Parsonage family home and boatyard on the north bank of the river and the glasshouse of the Winter Gardens and the Peoples' Palace in the background.

40. The *SV Carrick* was for many years a famous landmark on the Clyde opposite Carlton Place, itself an eye-catching part of the urban landscape. The ship, originally named the *City of Adelaide,* was involved in the Australian wool trade and is now being restored at the Scottish Maritime Museum in Irvine. While berthed in Glasgow, she was home to the Royal Naval Volunteer Reserve Club and also hosted regular gatherings of the diminishing number of members of the Capehorners' Club, skippers who had rounded the Horn under sail.

41. This scene from the south shows the extent of the commercial activity right in the heart of Glasgow as recently as 1950. Just across Clyde Street from the cranes is Glasgow's St Andrew's Cathedral.

42. A few yards further down-river is the famous suspension bridge linking Clyde Street and Carlton Place. Glasgow and Strathclyde University students are enjoying the Clyde Barrel Race.

43. Extensive engineering works were required to open the river to commercial traffic in the eighteenth century, and it was necessary to dredge the channel. Watching the dredgers at work was always a popular city centre pastime. This 1970's shot shows the dredger *Blythswood* and Hopper No. 27 working just down-river from the King George V bridge.

44. When the car ferry at Renfrew became surplus to requirements, an interesting new use was found for it—as a novel concert venue in central Glasgow. This conversion work is in progress in the lead up to the 1989 Mayfest. In the background is the *Tuxedo Princess*, a popular night-club in the early eighties, now departed.

45. At the Broomielaw the street and the river are busy in this early view taken from the Seamen's Institute. The dockside where the steamer lies is now the site of the Riverboat Casino. Nearby is the shiny new Atlantic Quay building, one of several new buildings growing up on the north bank of the river in the 1990s.

46. The passing of one era and the dawn of another. Before the arrival of a comprehensive road system, the river provided the main communication link between Glasgow and the west coast. It was possible to sail from central Glasgow to the Kyles of Bute and beyond. Here, the paddle-steamer *Caledonia* is seen on her last journey of the 1969 season as she heads down-river underneath the Kingston Bridge, an almost completed part of Scotland's growing motorway network.

47 & 48. A 1969 view of the Kingston Bridge under construction and a shot taken 25 years later as the bridge underwent repair. The repairs on the structure caused chaos in Glasgow; these aerial pictures give some idea of the size of this immense civil engineering project.

50 (*opposite*). Idiosyncratic sculptor, or scul?tor as he styles himself, George Wyllie's various creations have entertained the citizens of Glasgow and the Clyde towns from time to time. This is 1989 and the "vessel" is his famous "Paper Boat" described as the first to roll-on roll-off the Origami Production Line. Wyllie claimed the boat was intended to explore absurdities and ask questions like why an island nation made great because of the sea is now abandoning that role. After its launch it was taken to a berth at the Broomielaw, but subsequently ventured as far as the Thames.

49. In 1932 this was described as the new electric crane at Finnieston Quay. Since then, it has been one of the most dominant landmarks in the city, towering over the changes in the river over the last 60 years. This photograph also shows the North Rotunda, originally the entrance to the Finnieston tunnel, now a restaurant and casino.

51 & 52. The Finnieston crane hosts one of Greenock sculptor George Wyllie's idiosyncratic creations, a straw loco-motive. At the end of the display, the sculpture was deliberately set ablaze to symbolise the passing of Glasgow's industrial age.

53. Prince's Dock, Queen's Dock, Yorkhill Quay and Govan Dry Dock from the air in the 1960s. The number of cargo vessels loading and unloading just a few hundred yards from the city centre is impressive evidence of the Clyde's then commercial importance. In the foreground, cargo ships lie in the area which was to become the Garden Festival site. In the centre is the main course of the river and beyond is Yorkhill Quay, later to become the site of the Moat House Hotel, the "Armadillo" and the Scottish Exhibition and Conference Centre.

54. A vintage shot of Queen's Dock—with puffers tied alongside and steam tugs in the background. The *Kaffir* (right) was one of the best known of the Clyde puffers, often to be spotted around the holiday resorts "doon the watter".

55 (*opposite*). General Terminus Quay is where iron ore arrived for transportation by rail to the steel works of the Clyde valley. This picture also shows the old Govan vehicular ferry, and several examples of the pedestrian ferries.

56, 57 & 58. The *Glenlee*, built at Port Glasgow in 1896 and one of only five Clyde-built boats of her type in the world, was found in Seville and towed back to the Clyde in 1993. She had been renamed the *Galitea* and was used as a cadet training ship with the Spanish Navy in the 1920s. This three-masted steel barque now lies at Yorkhill Quay where she is being restored to her original glory by the Clyde Maritime Trust.

59. George Muir became something of a Glasgow legend as "Captain George" of Radio Clyde's "Eye in the Sky" helicopter. Here, in 1989, he stands ready for one of his regular flights to keep watch on road conditions for the city's commuters. In the background is the Pumphouse, which was converted to a restaurant in the 1980s. Captain George tragically died in 1997 at the age of 52 after an eight month battle against cancer.

60. Completed in 1998—just around the corner from the helicopter landing pad on the old Queen's Dock site between the Moat House Hotel and the Finnieston crane—this is Glasgow's newest concert and conference venue. Glaswegians, ever quick with a nickname, have christened the sleek, fluted steel structure the "Armadillo".

61. Just across the river from the Conference Centre and the Finnieston crane, this aerial view shows the site of the 1988 Garden Festival, part of a government initiative to regenerate the inner city. The intricate ponds, walkways, railway lines and docks of this hugely successful festival make a fascinating pattern. Despite a poor summer the Festival was generally accepted as a success, attracting more than four million visitors. In 1998, ten years after the Festival, the site is coming to life with the development of the Pacific Quay business centre and plans for a national science centre well under way.

62. Bell's Bridge, which was built to allow pedestrian access from the north bank of the river to the Garden Festival, has featured in more than its share of dramas. On one occasion it was closed because of flood damage to the installations on the bank, but this picture shows the *Waverley*, which ran into trouble by colliding with the bridge while being towed to Yorkhill Quay to have her boiler fixed in 1988. The *Waverley* lost one wing of her bridge, but the other bridge escaped with mere scratches!

63. The "Grand Union Jazz Salsa" aboard this Mississippi riverboat brought a real carnival atmosphere to the Garden Festival and a flavour of "Mardi Gras" to the city centre.

64. Symbolic of the demise of heavy industry on Clydeside, the cranes of General Terminus Quay were blown up in January 1981 and fell in seconds.

THE CITY TO THE
TAIL OF THE BANK

65. Even when the era of shipbuilding was at its busiest, there was a certain beauty and elegance about the Clyde. Against the latticework of the Harland and Wolff cranes and a dramatic sky, the Govan ferry makes its way across the river in the 1960s.

66. January 1966 and the Govan Ferry No. 7 completes its last journey. The crew has a touch of the "Vital Spark"!

67. Clearance under bridges was always a problem, making tunnels and ferries important. Many people will have forgotten the Finnieston tunnels which were opened in 1896 as an important link between the north and south banks for shipyard workers. There were three tunnels: one for pedestrians and two for horse-drawn traffic. In 1943, the tunnels closed to vehicular traffic and access was removed completely in 1986. This 1956 photograph catches the gloomy atmosphere of the tunnels.

68 & 69. Building the Clyde Tunnel at Whiteinch in the 1960s was a complex operation because of the difficult strata, ranging from rock to silt. The grim conditions in which the men worked are shown here, as giant cast-iron segments are bolted together with muscle power. The workers had to enter and leave the tunnel by compression chamber. Later, there were allegations that some of the procedures had been inadequate and that workers had suffered bone necrosis as a result.

50

71. Prince's Dock with the barques, *Moshula* and *Padua,* from the fleet of the legendary Scandinavian ship-owner, Gustav Ericcson, tied up across river from a cargo steamer in 1939.

70 (*opposite*). The beautiful full-rigged vessel, the *Grace Harwar,* was built in Port Glasgow in 1889. This is how she looked on the Clyde in the 1930s en route to be broken up at Rosyth. She often features in histories of the great clippers and was the last full-rigged ship in the world to round Cape Horn on regular service. She could complete the grain race from Australia to Britain in just 95 days.

72 & 73. Dockers always played their part in the Clyde's sometimes turbulent industrial history. Here in 1947, however, it is the army in action as Palestinian oranges and grapefruit are unloaded from the *Arnold Maersk* at Merklands Wharf. The 90,000 cases and 400 tons of fruit juice took around five days to unload! This shipment was a welcome treat for a population still living on wartime rations.

74. The dockers worked in all weathers, often without any protective clothing at all apart from a bunnet to keep the head dry. Here in the fifties a bunch of them enjoy a break round a brazier. In cold weather the "pieces" were heated on a toaster made from welding wire.

75. When Glasgow was a major manufacturer of locomotives, the Clyde was the starting point of the journey from St Rollox and Polmadie to the far corners of the Empire. A locomotive is loaded on board the *Clan MacLennan* at King George V Dock in April 1951 en route to Colombo. Another Clan ship lies in the background.

76. Stobcross Quay in 1933 and a giant locomotive from the North British works in Springburn is swung on board the *City of Barcelona* bound for India. The *City of Barcelona* carried seven of these locomotives, each, together with tender, weighing around 125 tons. Locomotives from the various Glasgow works gave sterling service in the sub-continent.

77. The bustle of the river in its heyday as a major shipping highway. Cargo ships on the move, dockers unloading at Meadowside and ships under construction in the background.

78. The last voyage of the *Captain Cook,* a famous emigrant ship which transported thousands of Scots to new lives on the other side of the world. Tugs strain as the ship starts down-water towards the open sea from Plantation Quay in 1959.

79. "Room with a view takes on a new meaning for people at Govan's new housing scheme", says the original caption. In the late 1970s, the Queen sampled some of the delights of the Govan walkway and called in on some of the tenants. The Singapore registered bulk carrier *Ocean Intrepid* passes within feet of the gardens.

80, 81 & 82. The Renfrew Ferry in three different eras—the first in the 1860s shows a steam-driven chain ferry in rural surroundings; the second, the 1950s model, looking across from the south side and, finally, the Renfrew-Yoker Ferry as it is today, a small passenger-only vessel.

83. This is what it was like beyond the gates of Fairfield's shipyard. The centrepiece of the picture is the *Empress of Japan*, while a Clyde paddler lies on the right and a military vessel is under repair on the extreme left. A tug tows yet another vessel in for attention at one of the busiest and most famous yards in the world.

84. Preparing for a launch at Barclay Curle's yard, the shipyard workers are seen here making up poppets—temporary wooden supports—at the stern of the *Kenya* in 1950.

85 (*opposite*). The sheer scale of manufacturing in shipyards could be awesome. Here the workers are dwarfed by one of the gigantic six-bladed propellers being fitted to the *QE2* at John Brown in Clydebank.

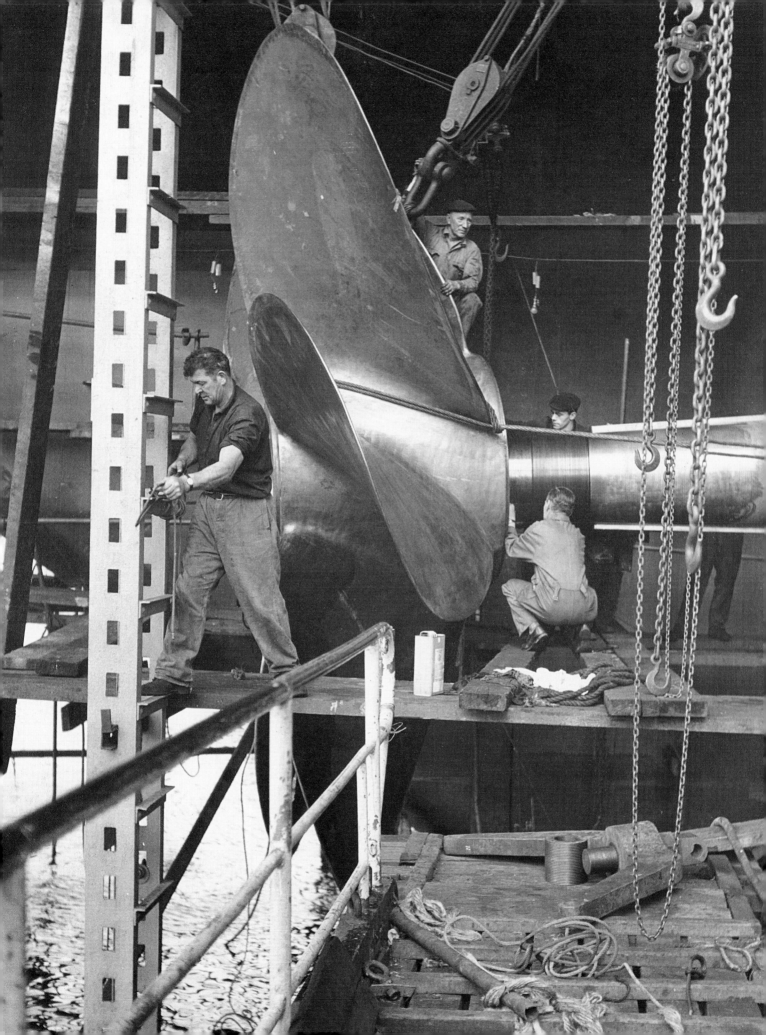

87. Another pre-launch routine. This time the workers are shoring up the interior of the bow with wooden pillars to absorb the impact as the ship hits the water during the launch. Launching giant liners was an incredibly skilled art, particularly because of the narrowness of the river.

86 (*opposite*). Many trades combined to build these great liners and create the accolade "Clydebuilt", a symbol of work of the highest quality. A driller (left) and riveter (right) work on the *Empress of Britain* in 1955.

88. The size of the individual parts involved in building a great liner is almost beyond imagination. Here an overseer, complete with bowler hat, and a couple of workers have a look at the *QE2*'s rudder as it is hoisted into place.

89. The Duke of Windsor in a hydroplane which Yarrow and Company were testing in the early twenties. Seated beyond the Duke is his equerry, Sir Harold Yarrow, while at the controls is Mr Charles Thompson, then Yarrow's Engineering Manager.

90. The modern face of shipbuilding on the Clyde. Frigates under construction at Yarrow's in 1996.

92. The Norwegian engineering group, Kvaerner, took over Govan Shipbuilders in 1988. A 56,000 cubic metre liquid petroleum gas carrier is seen here nearing completion.

91 (*opposite*). Glasgow's own ship, HMS *Glasgow*, impressive on a visit to the Clyde in 1983. A Type 42 destroyer she was built in Wallsend-on-Tyne, and served in the Falklands War.

93. Looking upstream to a smog-covered Glasgow in 1965, before industry declined and the Clean Air legislation started to bite. Construction is going at full tilt in the famous John Brown yard. Since the demise of the great yards, the riverbank has been colonised by warehouses and distribution depots.

94. Clydebank is synonymous with shipbuilding. In 1891, two naval craft are in a fitting-out basin, with the rolling Renfrewshire hills in the background.

95. A dramatic change as the river nears the Tail of the Bank. From the air, Rothesay Dock and Clydebank are in the foreground and the mountains of Argyll and the opening Firth in the background.

96 (*opposite*). The sheer scale of shipbuilding is accentuated in this view of the *Transvaal Castle* under construction at John Brown's in 1960.

97, 98, 99 & 100. Shipyard workers were a tough breed who turned out vessels which won world-wide admiration. Inevitably, there were industrial disputes, and this Second World War picture, above, shows workers leaving the yard on a "token" strike. The pictures below show workers heading for home—or pub—after a shift and looking even more cheery than normal on hearing the news that John Brown's was to build the *QE2*. The hazardous nature of shipbuilding is illustrated opposite as workers perch on flimsy looking scaffolding as the liner *Caronia*'s funnel is lowered into place in August 1948.

101 (*opposite*). Another illustrious moment in John Brown's history as a great Cunarder, the *Queen Mary*, is launched on 26 September 1934. Tugs strain and pull to get her into the correct position in the river which is littered by launch debris.

102 & 103. The launch of the *Queen Mary*, this time from the south side showing some of the thousands who flocked the rain-soaked banks to watch the mighty liner begin its life, and a glimpse inside the wheelhouse of the *Queen Mary* as workers put finishing touches to the steering gear and engine room telegraph.

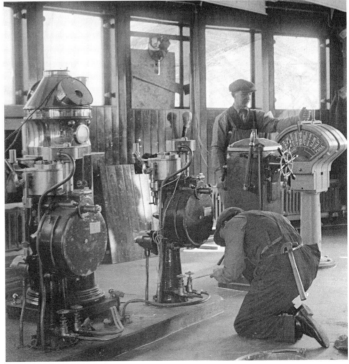

104. Now with her superstructure and funnels in place, the full beauty of the *Queen Mary* is apparent as she is eased out into the river to begin her journey down to the sea.

105 (*opposite*). This view shows how tricky it could be to take huge liners round the various twists and turns of the Clyde, in this case the Dalmuir bend. Note the flotilla of tugs working hard to keep the liner on the right channel.

106 (*opposite*). After the *Mary* came the first *Queen Elizabeth*. This striking photograph of the sheer of her bow shows the beauty and size of the liner. When completed the liner was secretly fitted out for use as a troopship. It wasn't until 1946 that she entered service with Cunard.

107 & 108. Only inches to spare as the *Queen Elizabeth* is manoeuvred on a windy day in 1965 into Greenock dry dock. No room for error in manoeuvres of this nature.

109. Arran's dramatic peaks form the backdrop to the *Queen Elizabeth*, at last in her Cunard livery, as she goes through her paces on the famous measured mile off the island's east coast just north of Brodick. Such spectacular runs up and down the Firth of Clyde were a regular feature as the great ships were put through their paces.

110. The last great Cunarder—the *QE2*—takes to the water in 1969 watched by huge crowds in the yard itself, on the liner and, as usual, on the other bank of the Clyde, sometimes the best viewpoint of all for these unforgettable events.

111 (*opposite*). Finally in the water—even un-finished, the beauty of the *QE2* is apparent as the tugs play their usual role of easing the vessel into the fitting-out basin.

112 & 113. The River Cart joining the Clyde opposite John Brown's provided vital extra width for the launch of these great liners. Above: The *QE2* is hauled towards the fitting-out basin. Below: On completion, she is edged out of the basin, a magnificent sight, illustrating the engineering genius and seafaring ability that enabled shipbuilding to thrive on such a narrow river.

114. Another of the Clyde's legendary yards was Fairfield. Like most of the other yards on the Clyde, from time to time it was stricken by industrial unrest. This evocative 1965 shot shows an official of the A.E.U. addressing a mass meeting in the engine shop as the once great yard was in its death throws.

115 & 116. A river which has seen countless battles fought and resolved, it faced its biggest challenge in the early seventies when workers at John Brown's (by now part of the Upper Clyde Shipbuilders, along with Connell, Stephen and Fairfield) occupied the yard in protest against the proposed closure. Right, the co-ordinating committee meets under the chairmanship of Jimmy Airlie (centre). Jimmy Reid is seated third from the left. Above, during the work-in, which ran from July 1971 to September 1972, the workers show approval and support for their Committee.

117. *Empress* liners were always particularly beautiful, and were favourites of Clydesiders. This is the second *Empress of Britain*, which was described in the original caption as "the most beautiful vessel afloat" when it was launched at Clydebank in 1930.

118. Built in Fairfield's, the *Athenia* sailed regularly between Glasgow and Montreal until her fateful encounter with a German U-boat. Torpedoed off the Irish coast, she was the first casualty of World War Two, sunk within hours of the outbreak. Of the 1,147 passengers and crew on board, 112 lost their lives.

119. The Clyde-built *Empress* liners rival the great Cunarders for beauty. This is the third *Empress of Britain* leaving the Clyde in 1956, at high-tide as usual.

120. The *Caronia*, tugs belching smoke and straining on the lines as they manoeuvre her in 1948, another example of the skill required to shepherd these craft down river.

121. Working in the yards was always difficult and dangerous. There were frequent accidents but it was surprising that there were not many more. Here in 1939, workers clamber over a caisson launched at Fairfield's. No lifejackets in sight, indeed one of the men appears to be wearing a bowler and the only concession to safety is a rescue boat circling in the murky waters of the river.

122. Steady nerves and a head for heights were absolute requirements for yard workers. Here workers are plating one of the upper decks of the *Sylvania*. If they had a moment to take their eyes off the task in hand, they had a wonderful view of the river, neighbouring shipyards and the rolling hills beyond.

123. The tanker *Foyle*, launched at Charles Connell's yard in the 1960s, was one of the largest ships built on the Clyde. This view once again shows, dramatically, the difficulty of getting such lengthy vessels in to a narrow river.

124 & 125. Clydebank was more than shipbuilding. The Singer sewing machine factory dominated the town for years, at one time employing more than 12,000 workers. The factory even had its own railway station and the Singer clock, a famous landmark, was reputedly the second largest in the world. The picture shows the workers flooding out of the factory gates as they head for home after a shift, on foot, by car, by bicycle and by scooter.

126. The German bombing raid on Clydebank on 13 March 1941 caused colossal devastation. Rescue workers hunt desperately for survivors in streets and houses turned into heaps of rubble: in two nights of bombing, 1200 Clydesiders died, more than 500 of them in Clydebank alone.

127 (*opposite*). This famous picture, one of the most evocative of the Clydebank blitz, is often used to illustrate the devastation and its effect on the population. The photograph was originally marked "passed by the censor for publication". Bombed out Bankies wander the blitzed streets heading for temporary shelter. The raids left only seven houses intact out of a stock of 12,000. Ironically a survey of Clydesiders a month before the bombing raids in March 1941 showed that only 30% of them thought heavy air-raids were likely. The unexpectedness of the events made the night all the more horrific.

128. The original private Health Care International hospital, an illustration of Government sponsored efforts to diversify the Clydebank economy, was the subject of great controversy and it became mired in financial difficulty and political argument. The impressive riverside building, now under new ownership as HCI Medical Centre, is symbolic of the changing face of Clydebank.

129. One of the Clyde's many tributaries is the Black Cart. Here, on a winter's day at Inchinnan Bridge, are several examples of the post-war passion for converting ships' lifeboats into cabin cruisers for messing about on the river.

130. Glasgow's old airport at Renfrew was famous with airline crew and passengers alike for its dramatic approach over cranes and docks. It was often said that the pilots could see what the crane men were having in their pieces! This 1954 shot of Renfrew shows the modernistic terminal building and the DC3 aircraft, also in the vanguard of style.

131. The last mass-produced car made in Scotland was the Hillman Imp, manufactured at the ill-fated Rootes plant at Linwood. Here, a convoy of them use the Erskine Ferry en route from Linwood to Stirling in 1964. The car plant was originally sited at Linwood as part of the regional policy in the 1960s. It closed in 1981 when economic policy no longer favoured government support for ailing industries.

132. Queues were inevitable at ferry crossing points as car ownership grew in the post-war years. A busker entertains the waiting motorists with his accordion.

133. The new bridge at Erskine eventually signalled the end of the ferries. This 1971 view of the nearly completed structure captures its imposing sweep.

134. The length of the completed bridge at Erskine is shown here in this panoramic view up the river towards Glasgow.

135. The Forth and Clyde Canal joins the river at Bowling, still a popular spot for houseboats and river lovers. This is how it looked in 1974.

136. Dumbarton Rock, with the world's last sea-going paddle steamer, the *Waverley*, cruising past.

137. Behind Dumbarton Rock, the River Leven comes down from Loch Lomond to join the Clyde. Denny's shipyard and some of the pleasure boats which ply the river can be seen.

138. William Denny & Brothers Dumbarton yard had a long history of innovative work. This was their Hoverbus, the first in the world, giving a demonstration of its capabilities before leaving for experimental service on the Thames. Hundreds of thousands of pounds were spent developing this hybrid craft but it was not a huge commercial success. The yard closed in the mid 1960s.

139. Denny dominated Dumbarton in much the same way as John Brown did Clydebank. This 1963 picture shows workers leaving the yard, pleased to put another hard day's graft behind them.

140. Helensburgh has long been a favourite haunt of commuters to Glasgow and day-trippers. An aerial shot from around the fifties shows the symmetry of this well-to-do town which was partially built along the lines of Edinburgh's New Town. The town takes its name from the wife of its founder, Sir James Colquhoun of Luss. It is also famous as the birthplace of John Logie Baird, inventor of television. Looking back towards Glasgow, Craigendoran Pier, now derelict, is seen with a Clyde steamer alongside.

141 & 142. The famous blue trains whisked Glaswegians down to Helensburgh for a paddle in the sea, a dip in the pool or even a ride on a pony! These pictures from the fifties show that, even before the days of the electric train, the beach was a magnet for day-trippers. Though some preferred to face inland!

143. Charles Rennie Mackintosh's Hill House was built for publisher Walter Blackie in 1902. Now restored to its former glory, it is a popular attraction for visitors to the Clyde. Handing over the completed building, Mackintosh said to Blackie, "It is not an Italian villa, an English mansion, a Swiss chalet or a Scotch castle. It is a dwelling house."

144. Yachting and Helensburgh are synonymous. Just along the coast, Rhu is a haven for the sailor. Here, the national championship of the GP14 dinghies is underway in the sixties.

145. Bathing belles at Helensburgh swimming pool. The original caption observes that "with blue skies above, who cares if it is wet at the bottom of the chute"!

146. Many of the beautiful ships born on the Clyde ended in the breakers yard at Faslane, in the shadow of the Argyll Hills. This poignant picture shows the last journey of the *Aquitania* as she is towed into the breakers yard in 1950. She had been launched at Brown's in 1913. The Second World War extended her life when she saw service as a troopship.

147. Another evocative moment as the aircraft carrier *Ocean* arrives at Faslane in 1962 to face the hammers of the shipbreakers.

THE TAIL OF THE BANK
TO AILSA CRAIG

148. The industrial landscape of the lower Clyde. Church spires mingle with factory chimneys above Greenock, looking back up-river over Port Glasgow.

149. Before improvements to the channel allowed vessels to make their way up-river, Glasgow had need of a port, a role once fulfilled by Port Glasgow. This is the town before the waterfront was re-claimed for the construction of the M8 motorway.

150. Early in the century, Port Glasgow's West Harbour shows how, even in those days, the river was an important recreational facility. Note the houseboat moored alongside pleasure vessels.

151. A modern full-scale replica of Henry Bell's *Comet*, the first commercially viable steamship in the world. The original vessel, built at Port Glasgow in 1812, dramatically reduced the six-hour road journey from Glasgow to the Clyde estuary, but she sank after hitting rocks in 1821.

152, 153, 154 & 155. Welder, Plumber, Plater, Shipwright—four of the trades that combined to create the great ships of the world. These are all Port Glasgow workers from Lithgow's in the sixties.

156. Waitress service, HP sauce, tomato ketchup, napkins at the ready! This was the Lithgow staff canteen in the days before broth, mince and tatties were usurped by burgers and chips. A period touch is the ashtray on every table—no non-smoking areas then.

157. Tugs have always played a vital role on the Clyde. Two famous names, *Thunderer* and *Flying Scot*, tow a huge semi-submersible from Lithgow's in August 1983.

158, 159 & 160. Echoing back to the demolition of General Terminus Quay in Glasgow, this sequence shows the loss of a famous Port Glasgow landmark—the Scott Lithgow crane. It required two attempts to reduce this structure to a heap of scrap metal.

161. A shipyard worker ponders his future following the take-over of Ferguson's yard, which resulted in many redundancies. In the background is the fifteenth century Newark Castle, where Mary Queen of Scots reputedly stayed after her defeat at the Battle of Langside.

162. A derelict monument to a bygone era. Considered an eyesore by some, the A-listed Gourock Ropeworks factory in Port Glasgow faced an uncertain future in 1998 after a planned conversion to flats was abandoned.

163. Not only is the Clyde famous for producing naval craft, its deep water estuary and adjacent lochs provide a perfect anchorage. Three ships of the First Destroyer Squadron line up off Greenock in March 1962.

164. On Lyle Hill above Greenock is the Free French Memorial, a combination of the Cross of Lorraine and an anchor. It commemorates the role played by the Free French Navy, many of whom were based in the town during the Second World War, and lost their lives in the Battle of the Atlantic. The French corvette *Aconit* lies at anchor in the Firth.

165. As late as the sixties, *Empress* liners were still sailing to Canada from the Tail of the Bank, often taking emigrants to a new life. A farewell from pipers triggered many a quayside tear. Scotland's regular liner link with the New World became a victim of the jet age.

115

166 & 167. Two views of the busy fitting-out basin at Scott Lithgow's yard in the eighties—naval vessels, submarines and rigs all nearing completion.

168. For many a shipyard worker, the enemy was the time clock. As yards closed and equipment was auctioned off, Lot 53 from a Greenock shipyard was carted off proudly.

169. The construction of a dry dock at Greenock's East India Harbour. The coffer-dam at the entrance has been completed and excavation is underway prior to laying the concrete floor. The dock completed a trio on the Clyde along with the Firth of Clyde Dry Dock and Barclay Curle's at Scotstoun. In the background is the characteristic skyline dominated by shipyard cranes.

171 (*left*). Clyde steamers tightly packed at Albert Harbour, Greenock, on completion of the 1953 summer season, with the well-known Clyde ship the *Maid of Ashton* in the foreground.

170 (opposite). Two favourites, the *Waverley* and the *Jeanie Deans*, pictured together in Greenock in 1975. The *Waverley* still paddles her way up and down the Clyde and makes occasional guest appearances for tourists on the Bristol Channel, the Solent and the Thames. Equally famous in her day, *Jeanie Deans* was only months away from being broken up.

172. Albert Harbour also played host to many naval ships, but the ubiquitous *Waverley* again gets in on the act as mine-sweepers prepare for a 1959 Royal Navy exercise, code-named Arran Pilot.

173. Scott's of Greenock celebrated its 250th Anniversary in 1961. *Warlight*, *Limelight* and *Skylight*, three of the Clyde's legendary coasters, "the puffers", are in dry dock awaiting repair.

174 & 175. Sugar-refining was an important industry on the lower Clyde. Above: packing sugar at Walker's refinery, Greenock. Below: bulk sugar being unloaded at the James Watt Docks in Greenock in 1959.

176 (*opposite*). The Greenock blitz began on the night of 6 May 1941 when about 50 German planes bombarded the town inflicting serious damage. Worse was to come the following night, when the whole town seemed ablaze. Curiously, as with the Clydebank blitz, damage to the shipyards was minimal. Over the two nights, 280 people lost their lives and, out of a total of 18,000 homes, nearly 10,000 suffered some sort of damage, leaving long-term housing problems for the town to solve.

177. Here Navy men enjoy a break for a smoke during demolition work in what the censor called "a west of Scotland town", in fact Greenock.

178. Firemen hose down one of many fires while the pawnbrokers' brass balls hang forlornly outside the destroyed building.

179. A historic picture of Gourock Bay from the turn of the century, before the railway station was built. Even in those days, newspaper marketing was big business. Alongside the quay is a hoarding, advising the world that the *Evening Times* had the greatest circulation of any evening paper in Scotland. Interestingly, the Renfrewshire hills have not yet been covered by the housing estates that now rise up from the river bank.

180. This early evening photograph captures Gourock's dominant situation on the Clyde, with the hills of Argyll in the background. The occasion was a Royal visit in the 1960s and the flotilla is composed of assorted naval craft, including submarines.

181. Gourock Pier in 1969 has a slightly chaotic look about it, with rail tanker wagons and assorted vehicles strewn around the quayside.

182. Gourock is still a major car ferry terminal for Dunoon. A Baby Austin embarks in January 1954. The Tail of the Bank's other crossing, operated by Western Ferries, runs from McInroy's point to Hunter's Quay.

183. Gourock Pier in the 1940s as huge crowds embark for the immensely popular trip to Rothesay and the Kyles of Bute.

184. In 1926, these hardy holidaymakers enjoyed the delights of Gourock's open-air swimming pool. Still open today, it is heated to 86°F: was the climate warmer in the old days or were they tougher?

185 (*opposite*). The magnificence of the *QE2* (the last Cunarder) is apparent during her speed trials off Arran in 1968. This legendary icon still draws admiring crowds from New York to Sydney, from Cape Town to the Caribbean. Port Glasgow-born Donny O'Rourke's poem, "Down to the Sea", captures the mood:

"Growing up on the Lower Clyde
Argyll was greener on the other side.
We watched the last Cunarder glide
Down to the sea."

186. Looking astern from the original *Queen Elizabeth* during her trials, again off the Isle of Arran.

187. Naval ships as well as liners trialled off Arran, and this dramatic and powerful picture shows the awesome HMS *Hood*. "The Mighty Hood" was sunk with the loss of 1419 lives by the German battleship *Bismarck*, off the north of Scotland in 1941. Then flagship of the British Navy, *Hood* had slipped anchor in Rothesay Bay to cut off the German battleship's escape from the Baltic to the Atlantic.

188. A remarkable picture of the *Queen Elizabeth* off Gourock as she emerges from battleship grey to the full glory of Cunard's post-war livery.

129

189. The Firth of Clyde—during the two wars and in the post-war years—was a vital conduit to the Atlantic for naval vessels from both Faslane and the Holy Loch. This picture shows small craft of the Reserve Fleet at Faslane with the aircraft carrier *Hercules* in the background. The area is now the main base for Britain's Trident nuclear submarine fleet.

190. The Clyde has witnessed numerous sea tragedies, one of the most dramatic being the sinking of the K13 in 1917 during trials in the Gare Loch. The K boats were huge, destroyer-sized, steam-driven submarines which were plagued by catastrophe: they caught fire, sprang leaks and stuck on mudbanks. The K13, with 80 civilians and sailors on board, sank after water poured into the boiler room. The desperate rescue attempt took 54 hours in freezing waters. A memorial to the six Fairfield's employees and 26 Naval personnel who perished now stands in Elder Park, Govan.

191. In the early days of the century, when large parts of Argyll were virtually inaccessible by road, Clyde steamers provided the main form of transport. Particular ships were favourites, often visiting areas where the piers have long since disappeared. This is the legendary *Lucy Ashton* at Garelochhead.

192. Kilcreggan, at the tip of the Roseneath Peninsula between Loch Long and the Gare Loch, was a regular stop in the heyday of the Clyde steamers. The pier celebrated its 100th anniversary in 1997 when this picture was taken. Nowadays the only service is the passenger ferry to Gourock.

193. Another great favourite with Clyde steamer fans was the *Jeanie Deans*, seen here at Craigendoran Pier on a dreich afternoon. Craigendoran is now derelict, a sad memorial to the great days of Clyde steamers.

194. The passion for sailing on the Clyde in pleasure steamers dates back to before the turn of the century. The *Lady Rowena* sailed on North British services out of Craigendoran. Built in Ayr, she was innovative in that the dining saloon was on the main deck, allowing diners to view the passing scenery.

195. The *Duchess of Montrose* and the *Duchess of Hamilton*, two very popular turbine steamers, plied the Clyde from Gourock on the Campbeltown run in the mid-fifties. This is the *Duchess of Montrose*, absolutely mobbed, as she sets out from Dunoon where even the steamer viewing area is busy. Hielan' Mary's statue in the background keeps an eye on the comings and goings.

196. Fair Saturday was the day when Glaswegians moved out of the city and headed "doon the watter". Long queues at the main railway stations throughout the day were a tradition. This is Wemyss Bay station on a Fair Saturday in the 1950s as the crowds leave the train and queue to embark the ferry. It may be July, but bunnets and plastic raincoats are all in evidence, as well as the usual battered suitcase!

197. Dunoon has always been a focal point for Clyde cruising. It's after the Second World War and there is barely an inch of space on the *King Edward* as it lands a full complement of passengers.

198. The ship's band was a regular and popular feature of Clyde steamers. Fiddle, banjo and box: the band of the *Queen Mary II*.

199 (*opposite*). The Cowal Highland Games are among the most important on the calendar and they are taken very seriously by all competitors, regardless of age. This dancer from Perth, the youngest in the 1959 competition, tongue between her teeth, concentrates on her footwork during the sword dance competition.

200. The HMS *Vanguard* is part of the Trident fleet, British successor to the Polaris nuclear submarines, and it too attracts the attention of protesters. These sea-borne CND campaigners attempt to inhibit the progress of the vessel as she arrives at Faslane in 1992.

201. The Holy Loch was a focal point for anti-nuclear demonstrations. In March 1962, protesters make their views known.

202. Seafarers dread the peril of semi-submerged rocks. This light marks the Gantocks, a string of rocks close to Dunoon Pier. The *Waverley* was one of a number of vessels to tangle with the Gantocks—she ran aground here on Glasgow Fair Friday in 1977.

203. The Cloch Lighthouse is an important landmark on the Renfrewshire coast. In 1933, these two six-metre yachts turn during the Clyde yachting season.

205. Rothesay Bay from the air, looking towards Toward Point and the Cloch lighthouse.

204 (*opposite*). An eyesore to many, yet an important navigational aid to yachtsmen on the Firth of Clyde, the Inverkip stack dominates the Firth and is visible from miles around. Despite the fact that the power station has been virtually unused since it was built in 1976, demolition of the chimney would not be welcomed by all. In a letter to *The Herald*, the Secretary of Cowal Golf Club noted that "it provides a perfect line for your tee shot at the twelfth hole"!

207. Puffers on a wet October afternoon in 1954, alongside Rothesay Pier with its distinctive clock tower.

206 (*opposite*). The rush hour in Rothesay Bay! One paddle steamer leaves, the car ferry arrives and the Royal Yacht *Britannia* is moored in the bay alongside naval craft, yachts and fishing boats.

208. The *Jeanie Deans* leaving Rothesay Pier, just after a fire which had destroyed the clock tower in 1962. In the foreground, a family returns from a "self drive" trip around the bay.

209. Rothesay's palm trees are a reminder that the climate in the West of Scotland, while wet, is also mild. The September evening sunlight creates a serene setting for submarine depot ship HMS *Montclare*, anchored in the bay in 1954.

210. Fishing from the pier was a fascination for youngsters and this group of would-be Mark Twains provide a typical scene from the 1950s.

212. Summer 1934 and the sun beats down on the canopied shop-fronts of Largs. A paddler stops off on one of its many Clyde cruises. The pier is now mostly used for traffic to Cumbrae, but the occasional fishing boat still puts in to unload its catch.

213. Along with fishing from the pier, playing with model yachts was also a great pastime. This typical 1930s scene shows the Largs boating pond, nowadays used for football and basketball.

211 (*opposite*). Largs, a douce town much favoured by retired people, is famous for day-trippers and traffic jams! This view over the town looks towards Great and Little Cumbrae, with the tip of Bute in the middle and Arran beyond. On the south side of the Great Cumbrae is the little town and pier of Millport, a favourite spot for holiday homes.

214. Largs foreshore early in the century; passengers disembark from a trip around the bay—resplendent in jackets, collars and ties, hats, coats over the arm and even a walking stick—a striking contrast to the Reeboks and casual look of today!

215. Easter Monday in the 1960s and the car parks of Largs are mobbed, while the rowing boats await an improvement in the weather.

216 & 217. No trip to Largs is complete without an ice-cream from Nardini's. In 1985, the palm court trio adds a touch of musical class to the traditional coffees and cakes.

218. The Pencil, commemorating the Battle of Largs in 1263, has been the focus for innumerable picnics by day-trippers down the years. Two Cumbrae ferries are seen making their regular shuttle from Largs Pier. The battle took place when King Haakon's fleet was blown ashore by a fierce gale. After two days of skirmishing he retreated. The battle is believed to have played a part in the return of the Hebrides from Norwegian to Scottish control.

219. Largs is proud of its Viking connection. This longship, though, had not come across the North Sea, merely from Inverkip marina. Crewed by men from the Shetlands, it was departing to take part in the Viking Festival in 1981.

220. Magnificent sunsets are a feature of the Clyde coast. Even industrial landmarks can take on a certain elegance, as shown here by the twin cranes of Hunterston Ore Terminal.

221. As well as liners the Clyde was the birthplace of beautiful yachts. Many came from around Sandbank in the Holy Loch. Fife's of Fairlie produced or designed yachts such as *Moonbeam*—seen here racing off Largs. In the old days such yachts were often crewed by Argyll fishermen who received the equivalent of around £1.50 a week!

222. Ardrossan is an important ferry terminal on the Clyde coast. Nowadays, it is used mostly for Arran traffic. However, in earlier years, as in this 1931 shot, it was used by large freighters, such as the *Jameson* seen in the background. In the foreground is the *Glencoe*, a MacBraynes West Highland ferry, which was laid up in Ayrshire in the 1930s.

223. Arran is very popular with holidaymakers—although not usually on account of the climate. However, this 1964 picture was originally captioned "heat haze hanging over Brodick beach"! No doubt there weren't any complaints from holidaymakers soaking up the sun and cooling off in the Firth.

224. The *Glen Sannox*, lying here in Brodick in 1968, transported thousands of Glaswegians from Ayrshire to the magical island of Arran. In the background can be seen the snow-flecked Goatfell.

225. It is impossible to mention Ayrshire without mentioning Burns. Looking down Irvine's Glasgow Vennel from Townhead in the early 1970s, the first house on the right hand side with the attic windows is where Burns once lodged. The restoration of the Vennel, part of the old drovers' road to Glasgow, won a Europa Nostra award in 1986.

226. Like Lanark and Rutherglen, Irvine has a long history of summer festivals. This is the Marymass Queen arriving outside the townhouse in 1959 for a day of celebrations. The origins of the Fair, organised by the Carters' Association, lie in the days when goods arriving by ship were transported by horse and cart to Glasgow.

227. Helicopters from the naval air base at Prestwick are a frequent sight around Ayrshire and the Navy is always ready to add some excitement to local attractions. This is an air-sea rescue demonstration in 1991 involving the Troon lifeboat at Irvine Harbour Festival.

228. Dominant in Troon harbour is the Ailsa Shipbuilding Company's construction shed. The ship in the stocks here in March 1986 was a car and passenger ferry for the Isle of Man service. In the foreground are gunboats for the Mexican Navy!

229. This massive audience, photographed at Prestwick pond on a summer Saturday in 1935, shows how important open-air swimming pools were to resorts of the era. Galas were a common feature, with comedy diving acts as well as swimming races and the inevitable beauty queen contests.

230. Huddled in the beachside shelter, lashed by surf and rain, families enveloped in raincoats get out the thermos flasks and sandwiches and make the best of it. The Glasgow Fair holiday in 1956!

231. Flying on holiday may now be the norm, but in the 1950s aircraft were still a source of wonder for many people. Here, a USAF plane lands at Prestwick Airport in the days before the bypass took the road around the end of the runway. Cars had to give way to planes landing and taking off.

232. Prestwick in a different guise. After the war, a succession of air shows brought thousands of spectators to the Ayrshire coast to thrill at the latest in aviation technology. Nothing was more exciting than the early days of Concorde. This is Concorde 01, the pre-production model, swooping low over the runway to the delight of the crowds in the 1960s.

233 & 234. The American cultural influence on Britain is captured in this 1950s picture of the US Air Force base at Monkton. Jukebox, sharp dressing and neat footwork: these early rock 'n' rollers are the epitome of cool . . .

. . . and there was none cooler than "The King", Elvis Presley, photographed at Prestwick on his only visit to the UK: a stopover on 2nd March 1960 en route home from Germany where, as US53310761, he was undoubtedly the world's most celebrated GI.

235. Ayr is an important market town, not least for fish, and the harbour is still used today by trawlers from Ayrshire and Argyll. This shot from February 1954 shows a Campbeltown registered vessel amid the industrial gloom of the era.

236. Ayr from the air, showing the many crossings of the River Ayr as it joins the Clyde estuary. This early 1990s shot shows the fish market with fishing boats alongside, a coastal steamer, a coaster on the opposite bank and the coal terminal prominent in the foreground. The cluster of industrial buildings beyond prompts the thought that, with riverside developments so popular, there is scope for change in Ayr.

237. Fish boxes, packed tight with the catch, in an icy-cold fishmarket in Ayr. Fishermen and salesmen, well-wrapped against the chill, cast their expert eyes over the catch.

238. The national bard, Burns, occupies a celebrated position in the centre of Ayr, a town he lauded for its "honest men and bonnie lassies".

239. With its fine beach, Ayr emerged in the nineteenth century as a popular seaside resort. A classic beach scene as mum captures the moment for posterity in 1955.

240. Sadly, heatwaves are not guaranteed. Here, in the teeming rain, two teenagers take consolation in a Coke and a ghetto blaster.

241. Ayr's other equestrian connections are the stables and the racecourse. Early morning at the beach is an ideal place for wannabe Scottish Grand National winners to exercise.

242. Traditional entertainment in 1985 as the donkeys at Ayr beach are at the ready to provide a memorable moment for their young customers.

243 & 244. Another famous attraction is Butlin's Holiday Camp at the Heads of Ayr, a popular holiday venue in the post-war years. This view captures the famous chalets, tennis courts, cable-car, kiddies' playpark and amusements.

245. Turnberry is one of the most beautiful and challenging golf courses in the world. Here, two top Irish amateurs, Joe Carr and David Sheehan, are in action in an international event. Turnberry's place in golf history was secured by the unforgettable Open Championship of 1977, won by Tom Watson. Watson's duel with Jack Nicklaus over the tough finishing holes has become a legend.

246. The striking form of Ailsa Craig, popularly known as Paddy's Milestone, is visible from almost anywhere on the Firth of Clyde. This view over the rooftops of the seaside town of Girvan provides an appropriate and dramatic full-stop to a journey which began nearly 200 miles up-river in rural Lanarkshire, but only 60 miles as the crow flies.